IMAGES
of America

FREEPORT-
VELASCO

IMAGES
of America

FREEPORT-
VELASCO

Brenda Laird and
the Freeport Historical Museum

ARCADIA
PUBLISHING

Published by Arcadia Publishing
Charleston, South Carolina

Printed in the United States of America

Library of Congress Control Number: 2017933088

For all general information, please contact Arcadia Publishing:
Telephone 843-853-2070
Fax 843-853-0044
E-mail sales@arcadiapublishing.com
For customer service and orders:
Toll-Free 1-888-313-2665

Visit us on the Internet at www.arcadiapublishing.com

*For my Lord Jesus Christ, who gave me Freeport-Velasco.
I wasn't born here, but I came as soon as I could.*

CONTENTS

ACKNOWLEDGMENTS

This book would not have been possible without my Lord Jesus Christ, who engineered all the events that led to its writing. He led me to Brazosport Independent School District and to a job teaching sixth-grade language arts and reading in Freeport. During the 30 years between August 1982 and May 2012, I taught and loved thousands of students and fell in love with their hometown. I'd like to say I adopted Freeport-Velasco as my home, but it's more true to say that it gathered me to its bosom. As I drove through the streets, year after year, I found myself feeling as if I were back in my birthplace of Helena, Arkansas. The similarities are strong. Helena has seen the death of its downtown area, just as Freeport has. Both cities nestle next to rivers: Helena beside the mighty Mississippi, Freeport at river's end where El Rio de los Brazos de Dios meets the Gulf of Mexico. I live in a home I bought in Velasco a few blocks from the Old Brazos River.

The long avenues of tree-shaded streets are the same. Most important, the passing of years spent in the presence of people who touched my heart made Freeport seem more and more like home. And so it became my hometown.

Finally, I met Freeport's historian, Nat Hickey, who told me Arcadia Publishing was looking for a writer to tell the story of Freeport's history. Without Nat's help, this book would never have been written. Nat introduced me to the marvelous collection of pictures Dan Kessner made and donated to the Freeport Historical Museum. Studying Dan's pictures opened up to me the wonderful world of Freeport's history. Having access to the huge collection of images stockpiled through the decades by the Brazoria County Historical Museum helped me to finish the job, along with curator Michael Bailey's unfailing help and kindness. Unless otherwise attributed, all images in this book are courtesy of the Brazoria County Historical Museum.

I am deeply grateful to Jeff Pynes, executive director of the Freeport Historical Museum, for the museum's partnership with me that resulted in this book. The embers of Freeport's rich and colorful history are fading as each generation passes away. I hope this book will blow a breath of air on those sparks to keep them burning.

INTRODUCTION

Moses Austin did not want to die. He wanted to return with families of settlers to the wide and broad land that would become Texas. He sensed the beginnings of something great in a land teeming with game, a land ready for the ranches and farms for which colonists longed.

But 59-year-old Austin felt himself sinking into death, so he called his 27-year-old son to his side. Stephen F. Austin had been born in 1793, soon after the birth of a long-dreamed-for nation. Moses asked his son to keep a father's dream alive, and then, on June 10, 1821, he died. Stephen was a good son. He found a boat in New Orleans. He must have loved the way the little ship took the wind in her sails, because he named her *Lively*. He filled her with passengers and cargo and took her across the Gulf of Mexico to the mouth of the Brazos River, landing in 1821.

The Mexican government owned the land, and had granted Moses Austin the right to bring settlers into it. Stephen Austin would become known as the "Empresario," Spanish for entrepreneur, because of his responsibility for settling the land he took over from his father.

The colonists landed on the eastern bank of the Brazos. While some moved inland, many stayed and founded the settlement that would be called Velasco. They lived there for a time in peace. Then the Mexican government passed laws restricting immigration into Texas. Mexico set up Fort Velasco, manned by around 250 men, at the mouth of the Brazos 150 yards from the Gulf of Mexico. They built a customs house and began collecting taxes on goods moved by the colonists up and down the river.

The settlers began to chafe under the taxation, and two years later, fired the first shot of the Texas Revolution at Velasco. In June 1832, furious colonists boarded the *Sabine*, commanded by Capt. Jerry Brown. They ran the schooner through the Mexican blockade at Fort Velasco. On June 22, a distant cousin of Stephen F. Austin, John Austin, walked with his men from Brazoria to Velasco, boarded the *Brazoria*, and came downstream. They attacked Fort Velasco on June 25. The Mexican soldiers manning the big mounted gun in the fort could not lower it enough to aim at the Texans' boats offshore or at soldiers on the ground. The Texans dominated the battle, which lasted 11 to 15 hours. Finally, a white flag was raised from the fort as Lt. Col. Domingo de Ugartechea was forced to surrender.

The year of 1833 was a hard one for the colonists at Velasco. The Brazos River flooded, causing extreme distress, including unsanitary conditions that probably caused the ensuing cholera epidemic. Many settlers died, nearly wiping out the town just 12 years after the colony was founded. But the embers of life in Velasco kept burning. In 1834, the Texas flag was raised over the American Hotel at Velasco. In 1834, the merchant firm of McKinney & Williams was set up in Velasco. In 1835, a mail route from San Felipe to Velasco was established. After battles of the Texas Revolution led to Santa Anna's surrender in 1836, he was moved from Galveston to Quintana near Velasco aboard the *Invincible* and was held prisoner in Velasco. Texas president David G. Burnett moved the capital of Texas to Velasco, where he and Santa Anna signed treaties ending the Texas Revolution. Then Santa Anna was sent to the United States.

A very sad time occurred for Stephen F. Austin's colonists when the Empresario died suddenly of pneumonia in 1836. He was only 43 years old. He was buried at Peach Point Plantation, but his remains were later moved to Austin. The founder was gone, but the Republic of Texas continued and moved through good and bad times as it became the great Lone Star State.

In 1837, a gale near Velasco destroyed a sailing ship, the *Belvedere*, which ran aground in high winds and was destroyed. Then, in 1838, a horse race track called the New Market Course gave settlers a taste of excitement on the site of the present-day Dow Plant A on the Dow "Thumb," which juts into the Brazos River. Fort Velasco had been abandoned, and the Archer Hotel opened in 1838 within walking distance of the Fort Velasco ruins. Steamships in 1840 traveled back and forth up the Brazos River to Washington-on-the-Brazos. Texas's annexation in 1845 by the US government made it the 28th state in the United States of America. In 1858, a railroad from Houston to Velasco went into business.

During the Civil War years, the 14th Texas Volunteer Regiment, commanded by Joseph Bates, was headquartered in Velasco. The Gulf of Mexico and the Brazos River near Velasco were busy with sea traffic. The USS *Midnight* and USS *Rachel Seaman* shelled Velasco in 1862. Then, in 1864, the *Chochua* captured the *Lowood* south of Velasco. Many other vessels were involved in Civil War conflicts near Velasco, including the USS *Antona*, the *Exchange*, the CSS *Mary Hill*, the USS *Queen*, the *Louisa*, the USS *Penobscot*, the USS *Arrostook*, the *Stingray*, the *Marion*, the USS *Kinco*, the USS *Penguin*, and the CSS *Granite City*.

One of the most famous vessels locally was the *Acadia*, which ran aground in battle, partially sank offshore, and left its boiler stacks reaching skywards, becoming a popular fishing site for decades after the Civil War ended in 1865.

During all this time, the location of Velasco at the conjunction of the Brazos River and the Gulf of Mexico left the colonists extremely vulnerable to hurricanes. One mega-storm after another blasted the tiny settlement: in 1837, 1839, 1853, 1866, 1867, 1868, 1871, and 1875. A hurricane in the late 1870s effectively destroyed Old Velasco and all city records. After the hurricanes in 1886, 1888, and 1891, the survivors decided to relocate the town four miles upstream at New Velasco. Everyone packed up and moved.

Finally, in 1900, came the hurricane that killed over 6,000 people on Galveston Island and nearly wiped New Velasco off the map.

One

VELASCO

A map of Velasco dated March 22, 1837, contains an ebullient description of the new community of Velasco:

> Situated at the mouth of the Brazos River upon the Gulf of Mexico within 56 hours of Steam Navigation to the City of New Orleans, is remarkable for its eligible situation in point of health, location, and commerce. There is no situation upon the whole Gulf coast, perhaps none in the world, believed to be more healthy. Its commercial advantages need not be dwelt upon when this remarkable fact shall be known—that within the reach of steamboat navigation upon this river, there are twelve Millions of acres of cotton and sugar lands of unequaled quality, one third of which is capable of making double the quantity of those staples now produced in the whole United States. The emigration to this country unexampled in the history of the world must produce these Staples in two or three years in such quantity that Velasco must soon become the second export city upon the continent. There is at present from 7 to 8 feet water upon the bar which is capable of great improvement with small expense and good anchorage within one Mile of the City sufficient for the whole commerce of the world. The receipt of two hundred thousand bales of cotton per annum at Mobile and five hundred thousand at New Orleans has made them the first and second export cities in the United States. The cultivation of one third of the good lands upon the Brazos between the 28 and 32nd degrees of North latitude is capable of producing four times that amount, all of which must be shipped from the Mouth of the Brazos. What a City must the storage, wharfage, commissions, brokerage, insurance, ganging, weighing, inspecting, sailors and shipping build up, all of which is produced by its exports and consequent imports. Velasco is already in a most flourishing condition, with a vast deal of shipping to and from it.

Surely Stephen F. Austin, proud father of Texas, would have loved this description of his colony.

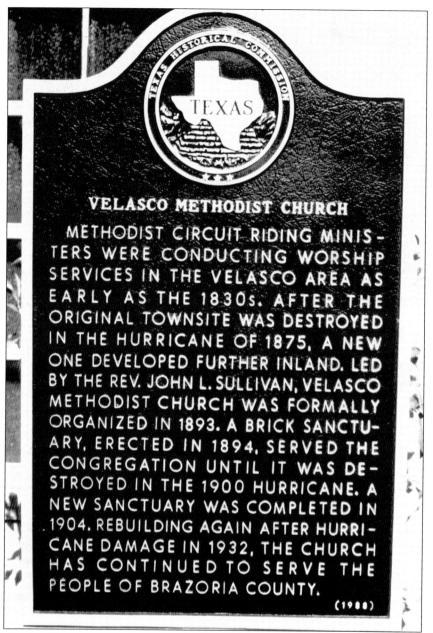

VELASCO METHODIST CHURCH

METHODIST CIRCUIT RIDING MINIS-
TERS WERE CONDUCTING WORSHIP
SERVICES IN THE VELASCO AREA AS
EARLY AS THE 1830s. AFTER THE
ORIGINAL TOWNSITE WAS DESTROYED
IN THE HURRICANE OF 1875, A NEW
ONE DEVELOPED FURTHER INLAND. LED
BY THE REV. JOHN L. SULLIVAN, VELASCO
METHODIST CHURCH WAS FORMALLY
ORGANIZED IN 1893. A BRICK SANCTU-
ARY, ERECTED IN 1894, SERVED THE
CONGREGATION UNTIL IT WAS DE-
STROYED IN THE 1900 HURRICANE. A
NEW SANCTUARY WAS COMPLETED IN
1904. REBUILDING AGAIN AFTER HURRI-
CANE DAMAGE IN 1932, THE CHURCH
HAS CONTINUED TO SERVE THE
PEOPLE OF BRAZORIA COUNTY.
(1988)

The Methodist Church provided a means for Old Velasco colonists to worship. The Texas State Historical Marker adorning today's Velasco Methodist Church at 320 North Avenue A records the work of Methodist circuit-riding ministers in Old Velasco. As early as 1830, they held services in Stephen F. Austin's colony on the Brazos River. The hurricane-harried colonists, having endured the destruction of their town again and again, moved to New Velasco. In 1893, the Rev. John L. Sullivan led his flock in the establishment of the Velasco Methodist Church. They constructed a brick building the strongest wolf couldn't blow down, but the winds of the hurricane of 1900 destroyed it. By 1904, the congregation had erected a new building that lasted 28 years. Then the hurricane of 1932 decimated much of Freeport and Velasco, including the Velasco Methodist Church. It was rebuilt, and the church has served faithfully ever since.

A plaque hanging from a pole in front of a substantial two-story house in Durham, Connecticut, says, "Here Was Born 1761 Moses Austin Whose Plan Led To Settlement of Texas By His Son Stephen." Moses was born on October 4, 1761, fifteen years before the birth of America. According to the State Historical Society of Missouri, his parents, Elias and Eunice Austin, who had nine children, died by the time Moses, the youngest, was 15. Moses had attended the small community schoolhouse in Durham for a time and loved books. He was able to start a merchant shop in Middletown, Connecticut, because of a loan from his brother Stephen. He opened a business in Richmond, Virginia, in 1785 after marrying Mary Brown. Partnering in 1789 with his brother Stephen, he bought a lead mine on the frontier of Virginia and was given the contract for putting a lead roof on the Virginia state capitol building. In 1793, Moses's son Stephen F. Austin was born and named for Moses's brother.

Moses Austin's tomb in Potosi, Missouri, says he died in 1820, but he actually left this earth on June 10, 1821. By that time, he had been through many ups and downs in the lead mining business. He had formed settlements at Mine au Breton, also known as Potosi, in Missouri on land granted to him by the Spanish government. His second son, James Elijah Brown Austin (called Brown), was born in 1803, soon after the Louisiana Purchase made that area part of the United States. Moses founded the port town of Herculaneum on the Mississippi River and endured terrible financial setbacks.

Here is a striking painting of Stephen F. Austin by Shari Hall Fullen Shelton. Austin came to be called the "Empresario," or entrepreneur. He had been a businessman with his father, in charge of Moses Austin's lead mine in Missouri. When the mine failed financially, Moses and Stephen started a bank in St. Louis. Sadly, that venture was a failure, too, because of the Panic of 1819. Eventually, they decided to leave Missouri and start anew in the Spanish territory of Texas. Moses petitioned the Spanish government for permission to start a settlement in Texas. At first, he was rejected. But because he knew Baron de Bastrop, a businessman from the Netherlands who had connections in the Spanish government, Moses Austin was finally given consent to form a settlement. (Courtesy of Shari Hall Fullen Shelton.)

When he knew he was dying of pneumonia, Moses Austin bequeathed to his son Stephen his grant, allowing him to bring 300 American families to the territory of Texas. Stephen's fulfillment of his father's wishes gave him the wonderful legacy of being remembered as "the Father of Texas." After arriving in Texas, Stephen Austin established Peach Point Plantation with his sister Emily near Jones Creek. The picture above shows his office and bedroom there after the 1909 hurricane and the one below after restoration. Austin worked in and out of this office, striving to find honest, hardworking colonists who would help him make the colony a success. (Above, courtesy of the Brazoria County Historical Commission.)

In 1936, Velasco city officials set up a monument at the Velasco Community House at the corner of North Avenue B and Skinner Street. It commemorates the arrival of Stephen F. Austin's *Lively* in Old Velasco in 1821, the fighting of the Battle of Fort Velasco in 1832, and the 1836 signing of the treaty between Mexico's Santa Anna and Texas president David G. Burnett.

FOUR MILES SOUTHEAST TO
THE ORIGINAL TOWN OF
VELASCO

LANDING PLACE OF THE "LIVELY"
FIRST VESSEL BRINGING IMMIGRANTS
TO AUSTIN'S COLONY IN 1821. THERE
THE BATTLE OF VELASCO, BETWEEN
TEXAS COLONISTS AND MEXICAN TROOPS,
WAS FOUGHT JUNE 26, 1832. A TREATY
OF PEACE BETWEEN TEXAS AND MEXICO
WAS SIGNED THERE MAY 14, 1836, BY
PRESIDENTS, DAVID G. BURNET AND
ANTONIO LÓPEZ DE SANTA ANNA BUT
WAS NEVER RATIFIED BY MEXICO.

The relationship between Mexico and Stephen F. Austin's colonists deteriorated through the years. According to the Texas State Historical Association, the Battle of Velasco opened the Texas Revolution and was most likely the first time blood was shed in the conflict between Mexico and its territory in Texas. Henry Smith and John Austin were in charge of the Texans in the fight. There were between 100 and 150 Texans in the battle and between 91 and 200 Mexican soldiers. Casualties are estimated at seven Texans killed and 14 wounded, with three of the 14 later dying of their wounds. Five Mexican soldiers were killed and 16 wounded. This is artist Don Hutson's sketch of the Battle of Fort Velasco. On the left, the ship *Brazoria* fires on Fort Velasco on June 26, 1832. (Courtesy of the Brazoria County Historical Commission.)

Col. Domingo de Ugartechea had to have been chagrined about the way the 11-hour-long Battle of Fort Velasco ended. He had been observing the Tejanos during the months prior to the battle and believed the Anglos were abusing Mexican land policies and being disrespectful toward the Mexican government. His request for reinforcements at the fort may have precipitated the battle. When the Texans tried to bring a cannon on board the *Brazoria* past the fort to use against the Mexicans in Anahuac, the Mexicans fired on them. The cannons in the fort had been mounted at an elevation to fire at ships. When soldiers on foot swarmed the fort, the cannons could not fire low enough to hit them, and the Mexicans were defeated. This pastel portrait of Colonel de Ugartechea was created by Anne Brightwell in 1975 for the Fort Velasco Restoration Society, one of many such portraits she made as she imagined how historical figures looked based on pictures and contemporary descriptions of the men.

James Briton "Brit" Bailey was one of a kind. He probably would have loved his notoriety. The Texas State Historical Association records his being one of Stephen F. Austin's Old Three Hundred colonists, his birth in North Carolina in 1779, and his death on December 6, 1832. Having survived the Battle of Fort Velasco, he died the same year, probably of cholera. His will is still in existence. In it he insisted on being buried standing up and facing the west. He may have included that he was to be buried "with my rifle at my side and a jug of whiskey at my feet." Some people say that he did. Others say that Brit's ghost still walks on Bailey's Prairie, taking the form of a round ball of light. The ball is called "Bailey's Light," and people say Brit Bailey is still searching for more whiskey.

Stephen F. Austin's work for his colony took a toll on his body. He traveled widely, seeking to ensure the quality of the settlement. He had been imprisoned in Mexico in a dispute that eventually played itself out in the Texas Revolution. Evidently, as with his father, Moses, his body could not take any more. In the home of George B. McKinstry, close to what is now West Columbia, Austin died suddenly of pneumonia at noon on December 27, 1836. He was only 43 years old. Grief for the Empresario was widespread. He was buried in what became Gulf Prairie Cemetery on Peach Point Plantation. Because of his status as the Father of Texas, his remains were removed in 1910 to the state cemetery in Austin.

Emily Margaret Brown Austin Bryan Perry, sister of Stephen F. Austin, does not look very happy in this picture. In many respects, including the burials of five children and losing her brother to an early and unexpected death, she lived a sad life. But there was happiness too. She married James Bryan in Potosi, Missouri, where Moses Austin had a lead mine. She and James had five children before he died in 1822. Emily remarried in 1824 to James Franklin Perry, with whom she had six children. They moved to San Felipe de Austin, Texas, on August 14, 1831. Then James and Emily lived with their children for a year in Chocolate Bayou, producing cotton and sugar, before finally moving to Peach Point. Emily died in 1851. James Franklin Perry and his son Henry both died of yellow fever in 1853. (Courtesy of the Brazoria County Historical Commission.)

Stephen F. Austin's sister supported his colonization efforts and was his sole heir. Emily was blessed with many Bryan and Perry descendants who have been and plan to be buried near her. She set aside land for a church and cemetery. The Gulf Prairie Presbyterian Church and cemetery outside of Jones Creek are lovely and peaceful. Emily would be overjoyed to see her descendants come together with the community to reenact Stephen F. Austin's funeral every year. Debby Collins, playing the role of her great-great-great-grandmother, wears a black dress and carries a bouquet of yellow flowers as she follows the coffin. Debby herself plans to be buried with her huge extended family near the matriarch of the clan.

Col. William T. Austin, a distant cousin of Stephen F. Austin, was the brother of John Austin, who helped lead the Texans in the Battle of Fort Velasco in 1832. According to the Briscoe Center for American History at the University of Texas at Austin, William Austin was wounded in the Battle of Fort Velasco. In 1833, the cholera epidemic that decimated the area took his wife, child, and brother. He had built a store, which was destroyed in the Brazos River flood that same year. In 1835, he was Stephen F. Austin's aide at the Battle of San Antonio de Bexar, later San Antonio, and wrote an account of the siege and battle. He was appointed collector of revenue for the port of Velasco in 1838. During the Civil War, he was a captain of the coast guard and a brigadier general in charge of state troops.

John Austin Wharton Jr., of Brazoria County, was a brigadier general in the Civil War. There were many Confederate troops in the port of Velasco from 1861 to 1865. Gun batteries on land kept Union ships from entering the port. Much war-effort activity kept the port busy. Cotton bales lining the docks were put onto European ships after guns were offloaded, along with medicines, ammunition, and supplies for the Confederate army and civilians. The Union ships fought hard to stop the commerce in the port. Some daring blockade runners made it through the Union ships and over the always-risky sandbars at the mouth of the Brazos River. One did not make it. The USS *Virginia* sank the *Acadia* between Old Velasco and San Luis Pass. Only its stacks remained visible. Its gravesite was a favorite fishing place for decades until it finally sank out of sight.

U. S. Life Saving Station, Velasco, Texas.

The Civil War had been over for 22 years when the Velasco Life Saving Station was established on June 11, 1887, as shown here. It was part of the Eighth Coast Guard District, which is headquartered in New Orleans. Today, the Coast Guard comes under the US Department of Homeland Security. The water transportation industry is a huge part of America's economy, with a revenue of $41.7 billion in 2013. The job of the Coast Guard is to guarantee the safety of everyone involved in shipping.

According to the US Coast Guard, when it was built in 1888, Life Saving Station No. 219 was located two and a quarter miles northeast of the original mouth of the Brazos River. On May 1, 1888, Joseph W. Simmons became the first Velasco Life Saving Station keeper; he was transferred to Galveston on November 24, 1888. At that time, Henry Tolland became keeper, and remained until his death on June 15, 1893. John F. Ahm was appointed head of the station on July 18, 1893, and remained in Old Velasco until his transfer to the Galveston Life Saving Station in 1901. John P. Steinhart, who took over on November 9, 1901, was still there when the hurricane of 1915 destroyed the Velasco Life Saving Station.

This picture, probably taken in the 1890s, shows fashionably dressed women and men posing in one of the Velasco Life Saving Station lifeboats, clearly enjoying an outing. The family of John Flores, who spent the summer of 1915 in Surfside, didn't go to the Velasco Life Saving Station for pleasure. In desperation, when the family was stunned by the massive hurricane, they went to the Coast Guard for safety. But the station itself was destroyed in the wind and storm surge, and most of the Flores family died. Only 16-year-old Maydelle Flores lived to tell the tale—at age 82, she recounted the horror of being swept out to sea. She rode monster waves all day and all night, and despaired of living. "God helps those who help themselves," she reminded herself, and made the final battle through body-slamming breakers to shore.

Here, in 1905, is the beach at Old Velasco, in present-day Surfside. All is peaceful and quiet. There is no evidence of the monster that the Gulf of Mexico can become. These young cousins are Roellers and Combses, two prominent Velasco families that intermarried. Edward F. Roeller, a photographer and businessman who would later become mayor of Velasco, took the picture of the carefree young adults who were his nieces and nephews. Behind them is the Surfside Hotel. It had been built in 1891, destroyed by a storm before it was completed, then rebuilt. Then the hurricane of 1900 drowned Galveston and decimated coastal Brazoria County. The big, lavish, strongly built Surfside Hotel withstood the storm, though it was heavily damaged and had to be remodeled. Later it was destroyed by fire. (Courtesy of the Brazoria County Historical Commission.)

Because the town was continually pounded by hurricanes, Old Velasco residents moved four miles upstream and founded a new town. In 1891, sailing ships like the barque *Carolina* could be seen docked, sails unfurled, on the bank of the Brazos at New Velasco. Anyone looking across the river from Velasco to present-day Freeport would see nothing except maybe a few cows grazing. The first building in New Velasco, shown above, was the train depot. Below, at the depot on July 11, 1891, a train waits for passengers or freight in a brand-new town.

There were two kinds of people in 1891 in New Velasco, just as there are in most towns. The steady, hardworking citizens did their work every day. Sometimes, they waited quietly at the train depot to catch the Houston & Brazos Valley train for a trip up to Houston. Then there were the "ring-tail-tooters," the saloon-goers like the ones below, who worked hard by day and partied at night. They were lounging in front of the Capitol Saloon, whose owner celebrated the fact that Velasco was the capital of Texas before a permanent location was chosen. Certainly, there must have been some steady men in this group. But contemporary accounts tell of gunplay and braggadocio like that portrayed in saloons in Western movies. The *Velasco Times* advertised the Live Oak Saloon and the Crystal Palace Saloon. The sheriff in New Velasco was a busy man.

There was plenty of work for those who wanted it. An 1893 *Scientific American* article, "The Great Jetties at the Mouth of the Brazos River," demonstrated the national importance of the deep-water port at the mouth of the Brazos. By 1899, the north jetty was 4,708 feet long and the south 5,018 feet. Repairs to the jetties in 1900, evidently after that year's hurricane, included placement of riprap and 5- to 11-ton stone blocks on the jetties. Years later, in 1935 and 1936, concrete caps were placed on the jetties, making them easy to walk on for fishermen. The people pictured below in 1909 dressed in Sunday finery are walking on the jetties before they were capped.

This is the office of the Velasco Brazos Land and Development Company, the syndicate that began the town of New Velasco. Ernest Dean Dorchester was one of the last managers of the syndicate. He had a big, gorgeous wedding cake of a house in Velasco. The river is visible in the far distance at center. Alta Florence Armstrong was a daughter of Martin Armstrong, who had a photography studio in Velasco in the early 1900s. She said, "The main corner of Velasco's business section was two blocks back of the syndicate building, which office was on high pillars. The river ferry operated around three or four blocks north. . . . The syndicate office was a two-story building with a gallery—where I saw my first typewriter in Mr. Anderson's office. (My father worked there once as a telegraph operator.)"

These pictures show Velasco in the early 1890s. Commerce was thriving. The wagons waiting to unload are full of cabbages from area farms. The dirt road was not muddy, so there had been no rain in the last few days. When the skies opened, the street turned into a quagmire. Then, drivers had to be concerned about getting bogged down in the mud or having wagon wheels come off. If the lady standing under the palm tree below wanted to go downtown, boardwalks would protect her skirts where they existed, but some areas did not have boardwalks.

Above is the Velasco Hotel in 1891. It occupied a city block between Avenues A and B within sight of the Brazos River near the present Velasco Bridge. Across the river was only forest where cattle grazed, because Freeport would not be founded for 21 more years. The huge hotel was luxurious, with a dome visible from a long way off. In the picture below of the dance pavilion, which was probably close to the river, the dome can be seen in the distance. The men involved in the syndicate promoting Velasco were proud of the Velasco Hotel and included its picture in their brochures, not realizing the hurricane of 1900 was on the way.

Above, a mother and her three daughters are seen in the Velasco Hotel. The picture is from the R.F. Roeller collection, so the women may have been Roellers. The picture at left shows Edward Frank (E.F.) Roeller in a bathing suit on the beach as a young man. There is speculation that the woman and girls may be his wife and children, but this is unlikely. He was born in 1881 and would have been about 10 years old at the time of the hotel picture. Also, the woman does not look like Ethel Combs, whom E.F. married.

Velasco was still a small town in 1896. It had just two streets, Avenues A and B, running along the Brazos River. But it was big enough for two photographers, E.F. Roeller and, pictured above, Martin Armstrong, artist and proprietor of the Velasco Art Gallery. From left to right above are Martin, Elmira, Alta Florence, Clinton Garnet, and Avery. At right is Alta Florence at 15 in 1900, when she had been selected Maid of Velasco. Something made Alta Florence bitter in later life about the way her father had been treated in Velasco. She loaned a picture of him to someone, having written on the back, "You might use it and give him credit for his work—the only 'honor' Velasco ever conferred on him."

SEPT. 11. 09

E.F. Roeller, a pharmacist, owned a building at Avenue A and Second Street. The street names were changed after Velasco consolidated with Freeport in 1957. South Second Street became DeZavala Street, and North Second Street became Caldwell Street. The picture below shows the drugstore's interior and evokes memories of hometown pharmacies with jars of candies and soda fountains. Roeller, a hardworking man, also became a photographer. Many of the memorable pictures of Velasco and Freeport are his. He worked at the Freeport Sulphur Company for some time. Later, he became mayor of Velasco. E.F. married Ethel Combs and became part of the extended Roeller-Combs family.

The *Velasco Courier* was one of many businesses thriving in Velasco in the early 1900s. There was Anderson Hardware, with horses and buggies parked out front while customers shopped inside. The First National Bank was in a big brick building. Men drove around in delivery trucks with their young sons perched on the seat beside them. Cotton bales were piled high on the Brazos River docks waiting for ships to pick them up. And then there was Skinner's Grocery. In 1892, Charles Skinner, who had been born in Exeter, England, married Kate Crain, who had come to Velasco in a covered wagon from Kentucky. The Skinners became a prominent family in Velasco. Charles became a director in the Velasco State Bank. His son Duke joined the bank as a bookkeeper, became bank president, and served on the Velasco City Council.

J.T. Dingle was a very successful man who began in Velasco and later moved his business to Freeport. Dingle's Hardware, Furniture, and Lumber Company occupied several buildings on Avenue A close to the Brazos River. A railroad track ran from the river docks to Dingle's. That was before the levee was built, and the train seemed precariously close to the river before curving inland to J.T. Dingle's buildings. His store is pictured here as it looked in 1912. The interior was pristine, with many merchandise-filled glass cases. Dingle had a pleasure boat named the *Lillian* that he took out on the Brazos River. He built a lovely two-story house on Avenue A in 1890. The house stood for seven decades after surviving the hurricane of 1900, but was destroyed by fire in the 1970s.

PLAYING BASKET BALL IN THE WINTER AT VELASCO TEX

The Combs family was prominent in Velasco. Ethel Combs married E.F. Roeller. Philip Combs was a cashier at Velasco Bank from 1919 to 1935. Lt. Arthur Combs served his country in both World War I and World War II. This picture shows the Combs House on Avenue A before the hurricane of 1900. Women in long skirts are playing basketball in the wintertime. Basketball was quite the rage. The Combs house was damaged in the storm. For some reason, it was decided to move it across the street, where it was bought and restored by Dan and Carolyn Tarver. The Charles Skinner house is on the right. This house remained where it was and burned down in 1928.

This picture shows the Velasco School in the early 1900s. This group of students may have included Alta Florence Armstrong and her siblings. It is possible that the photograph was taken by her father, Martin Armstrong, who would have kept the negative in his Velasco Art Gallery building. The names of the teachers at the school are unknown, but it is known that some of them had beaux, including a young man who worked at the shoe shop in town. The very idea of air-conditioning did not exist when teachers started school in September wearing long dresses and petticoats. Their sweat mingled with chalk dust; sweaty fingers left their marks on textbooks. The windows would have been wide open for any breeze that might have come down from the river several blocks away. In hard circumstances, the teachers taught well, and the students learned.

According to *Velasco Drainage District 1908–1991* by Ralph W. Gilbert, the Velasco Drainage District was established in 1908 to build and maintain levees to provide protection from Brazos River flooding. The original boundaries of the district were, on the south, the Gulf of Mexico; on the east, Oyster Creek; on the west, Buffalo Camp Bayou; and on the north, the Retrieve State Farm. The levee system had been constructed four years prior to the disastrous flood of 1913, the worst on the Brazos River in the 20th century. This picture shows levee construction that took place in Velasco in 1914 and 1915, evidently to repair damage done to the levee by the flood. As of 2017, George Kidwell is the chairman of the Velasco Drainage District, which continues to maintain the levee system at a standard that will protect citizens from flooding.

The port of Velasco was important from the very beginning, as was the shipping that entered it. Stephen F. Austin and his Old Three Hundred could move to Velasco because of the incursion of the Brazos River into Texas land. Shipping in and out of the port put the town on the map. This picture was taken in 1911 and shows an unidentified ship steaming majestically into the port of Velasco. Not visible are the sand bars that lay at the mouth of the river. The Brazos drains a lot of Texas land, and in 1911, it deposited a great deal of it as sand not far from the ship's wake. This made entering and exiting the river's mouth difficult for shipping. The problem would be dealt with decisively in 1929.

The Brazos River itself—*El Rio de los Brazos de Dios*, or the River of the Arms of God—has been deeply important to the well-being of Velasco's citizens. The picture above shows a group of African American children on the peaceful banks, enjoying the trees whose roots are well-watered by the river. At right, a young boy stands on the riverbank holding a raccoon.

This is H. Bascom Simpson in 1916. He had come to Velasco in 1915 to become superintendent of schools. He had to wait while the mud and cow droppings were cleaned out of the school after the hurricane of 1915. Soon he settled into a three-year tenure, during which he had a profound influence on the community. This picture shows the car he bought second-hand to ferry his girls' basketball team to games. The muddy after-rain trips provided many adventures. Sometimes the girls received extra training when they had to walk behind the bogged-down car. Simpson took a summer job at the Freeport Sulphur Company and never went back to superintending school. The difference in pay evidently was too great. Simpson wrote hymns for his church and sang in the Freeport Friendly Singers. He loved honey and bought it by the bucketful from an area beekeeper.

OFF For The Gulf At
Velasco Texas

One way the Brazos River provided for the well-being of the citizens of Velasco was by giving them a ready source of recreation. This picture, taken in 1900, shows people "Off for the Gulf" at Velasco. It must have been an exceedingly calm day, because ladies and men are perched in their Sunday finery on the top of the boat's cabin, and the river is flat and quiet. The date sparks a sense of unquiet, because the Gulf was going to play a dirty trick on Velasco in 1900. The house on the far shore is in Velasco, because Freeport would not exist for 12 more years. The boat would be traveling down through the jetties, past the US Life Saving Station, and out into the rougher waters of the Gulf.

Another way the Brazos River benefited those who lived on its banks was by giving them a livelihood. This is the party boat *Monarch*. Its captain would pick passengers up at the docks and, for a fee, take them out on the river. The boat on the previous page was very likely also an excursion boat. The passengers in this picture, taken in the 1900s, are all dressed up, while the captain is dressed to work. There were other boats working along the Brazos River. S.H. Hudgins and his sons established the Brazos Transportation Company in the early 1900s. They had a whole fleet that plied the Brazos taking passengers wherever they needed to go. Once Freeport was born, the *Thelma*, the *Hustler*, the *Idlewild*, and *Velasco No. 1* through at least *Velasco No. 7* carried passengers back and forth to Freeport.

This is Philip Combs, a member of the extended Roeller-Combs family that was so prominent in Velasco. Combs served as a cashier at the Velasco State Bank from 1919 to 1935. Charles Skinner was a director in the bank. His son Duke Skinner joined the bank as bookkeeper in 1924, when Philip Combs had been there for five years. Duke Skinner later became bank president. The bank started on Front Street, where its proximity to the river made it easy pickings. It was robbed three times. The 1932 hurricane had destroyed so many buildings around the bank that it stood nearly alone. In 1936, the bank was moved from its isolated riverside setting to a better location on South Second Street. In 1948, it was moved again to 304 South Avenue A. The building still stands and is now used as a residence.

Taken in the 1920s, this photograph shows a young boy and man in a delivery truck. The truck looks a lot different from today's pickups and 18-wheelers, but it got the job done. What the man and boy were transporting is unknown. There were many small businesses in Velasco. They may have been delivering merchandise from J.T. Dingle's Lumber, Hardware, and Furniture Company to a customer. Dingle himself may have needed a new case to show his wares inside his hardware store. Or maybe E.F. Roeller needed something for his pharmacy. Many businesses were thriving in Velasco, and any one of them may have hired this man and his truck. It would have been a little boy's delight to get to go to work with his dad and share in his work for a day.

Here is the interior of the Hudgins Bros. Feed Store. There were many horses and livestock in the Velasco area needing to be fed. This store provided that food in abundance. It also probably served as a gathering place for area ranchers and farmers, a place to catch up on the latest news and find out whose horse had thrown him and who had some good livestock for sale. The blacksmith was probably located nearby. If the owner of the feed store was a relative of S.H. Hudgins, who, with his sons, owned the Brazos Transportation Company, he was part of a very hardworking family. The picture shows a man among stacked bags of feed. Like all enterprises, this one was subject to the vagaries of weather. The hurricane of 1932 destroyed the feed store.

This photograph, taken in January 1941, shows Mayor E.F. Roeller (first row, second from right), Duke Skinner (first row, far left), and the other members of the Velasco City Council. This was 16 years before Velasco consolidated with Freeport in 1957. Some citizens of Velasco believed that the twin cities facing each other across the river should follow the example of two other cities up north. Minneapolis and St. Paul, Minnesota, together are called Minneapolis–St. Paul, and some believed that, when Freeport and Velasco consolidated, the new town should be called Freeport-Velasco, hence the title of this book. They were voted down, and the smaller town took on the larger town's name. The numbered streets in Velasco, since Freeport also had numbered streets, were given new names, mainly those of historical figures important to Velasco. (Courtesy of the *Brazosport Facts*.)

Two

FREEPORT

In the years preceding 1912, men looking for oil discovered sulphur deep down in a salt dome that would be called Bryan Mound. Overnight, the founders of Freeport laid out a cigar-shaped town. It stretched only two streets deep along the Brazos, the twin of Velasco, another two-street-deep town across the river. The outbreak of World War I soon after the discovery of sulphur at Freeport gave the new town great importance. The yellow powder buried under the earth was immensely valuable in America's fighting in the war.

The Freeport Sulphur Company arranged for the Tarpon Inn to be built on Second Street at one end of the long rectangle that was to be downtown Freeport. The two long streets were named East and West Park Avenues. They were intersected halfway by Broad Street. At the other end of downtown, on Fourth Street, the railroad depot was erected, the arrival and departure point of trains transporting passengers from Velasco to Freeport and out to Bryan Mound.

The sulphur was loaded onto Freeport Sulphur Company ships at the company's docks on the Brazos River. Then it was shipped out through the port, which had been a "free port" since Stephen F. Austin's days, without docking fees or taxes.

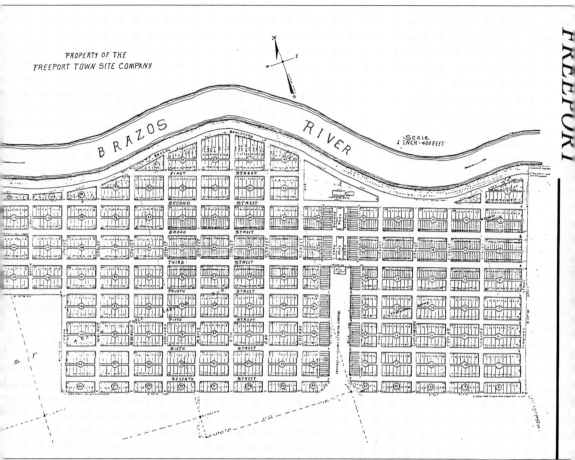

In 1912, the forest across the Brazos River from Velasco was cleared enough to be surveyed. The Freeport Townsite Company office was the first building in Freeport. It later became a Bell Telephone office and still exists on Broad Street. The Freeport Townsite Company did not plan a cigar-shaped town. The picture shows the dimensions of the town they did envision, although it took many years to grow into the planned shape. Frank Vanderlip was one of the businessmen who created Freeport. Vanderlip worked for the *Chicago Tribune* as its financial editor, and while William McKinley was president, served as assistant secretary of state. At that time, Vanderlip helped to finance the Spanish-American War by raising $200 million in bonds. He served as a founder and president of the Federal Reserve System and as president of the forerunner to Citibank.

Mischief Domineer
Bred by F. K. Belden, Horton, Kansas

Quiet Blanchard 15th
Bred by G. M. Scott & Sons, Rea, Mo.

Rex Domino
Bred by E. W. Johnson & Sons, Elk Xa

Gaston Woodford
Bred by Sen. J. N. Camden, Versailles, Ky.

Six First Prize Bulls

McCormick Mixer
Bred by Henry W. Marshall, Ea. Texas
This bull was Junior Champion at the Sesquicenten...

TYPICAL S.M.S. RANGE BULLS

Cattle have always been important in Texas, and the cattle in this picture were very important to Freeport. They were used as collateral in financing the Freeport Sulphur Company. If S.M. Swenson, owner of the Freeport Sulphur Company, had not first owned these registered Herefords of the Domino strain, he may not have been able to raise the money to pay for the extraction of sulphur from under Bryan Mound. He risked his prize cattle in the venture, and his gamble clearly paid great dividends. Another cattleman well-known to early Freeporters was R.E.L. Stringfellow. He ran cattle on both sides of the Brazos River long before Freeport existed. He and his wife, Nannie, were prominent citizens in Freeport for decades. After his death, she gave to Freeport the fountain that still beautifies the downtown park.

Freeport was a company town, built by the Freeport Sulphur Company. This 1912 picture shows the Freeport Hospital the company provided for its employees. The extraction of sulphur from under the earth was a dangerous process, involving boiling water that transformed a stone that could be ignited, sometimes called "brimstone," into molten sulphur. The yellow substance must have been extremely painful when it burned the young men who brought it out of the ground. The Frasch process used to extract the sulphur included pumping molten sulphur into several-story-high forms, where it solidified. Then the solid yellow block was dynamited to prepare it to be loaded, first into railroad cars and then into ships. Every step of the process was dangerous. It is no wonder that the company wanted a good hospital ready to deal with any trauma its workers endured.

This is downtown Freeport several years after its founding. The view is of Broad Street looking west from Park Avenue. Horses and a wagon await an owner who may have gone into the Freeport Pharmacy. Or he may have had business at the Freeport National Bank, the two-story building behind the horses. The bank was built in 1913 as a single-story building. Later, a second story was added for the Freeport Sulphur Company offices. This building still stands in downtown Freeport. To the right, out of sight, is another building that still stands. This was the J.J. Baker Barber Shop building, built in 1918. Over the doorway is the inscription "19 Baker 18," keeping alive the barber's name nearly 100 years later. The present address of the Baker building is 220 West Park Avenue.

This picture of the Tarpon Inn, built by the Freeport Sulphur Company, was taken in the 1930s or 1940s. By then, the hotel was a Freeport institution, and many grieved over its demolition in the 1950s to build a shopping center. Its glory began in 1912, when Texas governor Oscar Branch Colquitt and many distinguished men and women came to celebrate the birth of Freeport. The hotel had private baths in many of its 30 rooms and the best things available for guests at that time: electricity, hot and cold running water, steam heat, and transportation to and from Velasco across the Brazos River. The dining room was excellent. The hotel became a mecca for fishermen from all points of the compass and, for local people, the place to go to have fun and to entertain visitors and friends.

The photograph above was taken looking down West Broad Street in the early 1920s. On the right is the First National Bank building with the Freeport Sulphur Company on its second floor. The Freeport Pharmacy sign is barely visible over the rooftops to the left. The photograph below was taken in 1912. It also shows Broad Street but this time on its east end. Two automobiles are passing each other at the intersection of East Broad Street and East Park Avenue. The newly planted park between East Park and West Park Avenues is protected from cattle by a wooden fence. The Tarpon Inn is in the background.

The Tarpon Inn attracted sports fishermen from far and wide because of Freeport's location on the Brazos River, with easy access through the jetties to the Gulf of Mexico. People were also drawn to Freeport because of its proximity to sandy beaches right on the edge of the Gulf. In this E.F. Roeller photograph taken in the 1920s, one can almost hear the waves and smell the salty, fishy, beach smell enjoyed by these two women and a child.

Mankind's yearning for God manifested itself right away in the new town. By 1915, there were at least three churches of different denominations in the three-year-old town, even though there were still only a few streets, a few houses, and a few businesses. The Baptist church shown here was built at 331 West Second Street. The roadway may have been only dirt, but the church was solidly constructed, and its members must have been very proud of it. So too were the members of the Presbyterian church built right down the block at 402 West Second Street, and the Methodists, who also built their church in the 400 block of West Second Street. In 1926, St. Mary Star of the Sea Catholic Church was built at the corner of Velasco Boulevard and West Sixth Street.

In 1916, the City of Freeport spent $25,000 to build its first high school at 102 Ash Street, right next to the Brazos River. To protect it from flooding, the three-story school was built up very high, with a vast flight of steps leading up to the building. When a new Freeport High School was built in the 1930s, this building was used as the junior high school. By 1951, the Freeport school system had consolidated with the Brazosport Independent School District (BISD). That year, the stone structure became a maintenance facility for BISD. School buses were also parked there. The building was later sold and became a Gore Fish Industry marine service facility. Finally, having become too old to be trustworthy, the building was condemned and torn down. Freeport photographer J.P. McDonald took this picture.

While the people of Freeport were adjusting to life in their new town, so was the company that started it all. The year that the City of Freeport built its first high school next to the Brazos River, the Freeport Sulphur Company was busy shipping its product. Pictured is the four-master *Florence Howard* docked on the Velasco side of the river. The sailing vessel was used to carry sulphur to markets. Through the years, Freeport Sulphur would purchase many more vessels, naming them with numbers, starting with *Freeport Sulphur No. 1*. The ships changed with the times, becoming more like the ones seen today. While the *Florence Howard* was operating, sailors swarmed over her just as land-based workers were pouring into the sulphur company.

In 1913, these five men, ranging from young to well-seasoned, are on their way to work at the Freeport Sulphur Company. They are holding their lunch pails, which may have held greens, cornbread, and "pot likker," the liquid derived from cooking fresh-out-of-the-ground greens with salt pork. The third man from the right is Bryan Lamar Perry, born in 1891, grandfather of Debby Collins, who first showed the author this picture. He was the great-grandson of Emily Margaret Austin Bryan Perry and is buried near her in the Gulf Prairie Cemetery, close to his great-great-uncle Stephen F. Austin's original grave. Debby tells the story of her grandfather's carrying his six-month-old baby down the street as he sought refuge at the Schuster house during the hurricane of 1932. The wind was so great that it blew Perry's son right out of his arms, though the infant came to no harm. Perry himself died later that year of unrelated causes at the age of 41.

In the early 1900s, as men searched for oil, they came upon a mound in the earth that would later be named Bryan's Mound for the family that owned the land. Within this salt dome was found sulphur, the valuable yellow chemical that caused the creation of Freeport. But oil was found, too. It was a disappointment, because the drillers were looking for hugely producing wells, but the trickles were lucrative enough.

In *The Stone That Burns*, William Haynes told the story of the American sulphur industry. It all started with a man named Herman Frasch, who was trying in the 1890s to figure out how to get sulphur out of its hiding place in the ground. The world needed sulphur for explosives, for medicines, and for many uses that Frasch could not foresee, like tires, steel, and rayon. What Frasch could envision was a way to bring the sulphur up from under hundreds of feet of earth. His process involved pumping boiling water down to melt the sulphur, then bringing the molten liquid up. This picture, taken in 1915 by E.F. Roeller, shows his five-year-old daughter Mary Louise sitting with her doll on the first solidified stalagmite of sulphur brought up from under Bryan Mound.

The picture above shows the wooden framework for a sulphur vat being constructed in the 1920s. Molten sulphur was pumped into the vat until a giant block was formed. The great mass must have been beautiful with the sun shining on it. Freeport wasn't El Dorado, but the chunks of solid yellow were intensely valuable. Notice how level the top surface of the slab is. Imagine the hot liquid lying under the hotter sun before it solidified. According to Michael Bailey of the Brazoria County Historical Museum, the yellow sulphur was so bright that sunglasses had to be worn to prevent snow blindness. The image below shows a dramatic cut in the side of a sulphur stack.

These seven men were a team responsible for performing an exceedingly dangerous job. This is the dynamite crew, and they are setting charges in the sulphur pile. The goal is to blow a fixed section of it to powder so it can be picked up by other squads of men (and stay whole of body themselves). Notice the man holding the tall metal rod. A man on another dynamiting crew, Phineas Gage, the foreman of a railroad construction crew in 1848 near Cavendish, Vermont, once had an interesting experience with a similar rod. Another man had loaded the explosive, then tamped it with the rod. The dynamite blew, and the rod flew through Gage's skull, leaving a hole. Gage lived, and scientists studied his brain through the hole. This is a story none of the men in this picture wanted to live out.

After the dynamiters safely finished their jobs, this crew took over to get the powdered sulphur into railroad cars, which would then be pulled by a locomotive up onto the loading docks on the Brazos River to be transferred to Freeport Sulphur ships. The cranes themselves were remarkable pieces of machinery, with the ability to reach out and grasp the chunks of sulphur and to swivel and turn and drop them into the railroad cars. Skilled heavy equipment operators have always been valuable; the Freeport Sulphur Company bosses must have loved these men. Notice their long sleeves. Powdered brimstone can cause burning and irritation on the skin. That plus the hot Texas sun would have been enough to induce these men to cover up.

Railroad tracks were a common sight on Bryan Mound, as were railroad cars. This Freeport Asphalt Company car was photographed in the 1920s at rest on the tracks. Many chemicals were needed to carry on the business of the Freeport Sulphur Company, and this car carried one of them. Someone stenciled and painted the name with pride on the massive car, and included the designation "F.A.X. 613." Crews of men laid the tracks, and other groups—or perhaps the very same men—maintained them. The wooden ties and metal rails had to endure multiple hurricanes that roared in from the Gulf, along with the accompanying torrential rains. The crews who maintained the tracks under this car had their work cut out for them, as did all the men who carried on the business at Bryan Mound.

These are the Freeport Sulphur Company loading docks, with one of the *Freeport Sulphur* ships taking on sulphur and a tug boat alongside her. The engineer who drove the railroad cars up the mountainous scaffolding of the docks had to have nerves of steel. The engineer had to be a sober-minded, calm man who simply did his job, drove the cars up the precipitous slope, waited until they were unloaded, and backed them back down, then did it again.

This aerial view of Bryan Mound shows the Freeport Sulphur Company in the 1930s. By this time, nearly all the sulphur under the mound had been brought to the surface. Things would change drastically at Bryan Mound. Changes were happening all over Freeport. Men were considering diverting the mouth of the river. Events in the world were also having an effect on the twin cities astride the Brazos River. The onslaught of the Great Depression had tightened everyone's belts and brought a determination to make do with very little. Airplane travel had become commonplace, as evidenced by the small plane seen here. Events in the world were boiling up to create a shower of brimstone called World War II, though no one in Freeport or elsewhere in the world knew exactly what would happen.

The Brazos River, pictured after the flood of 1928 as it wound sweetly through Velasco and Freeport, brought both good and bad to the twin cities. The safe haven for ships brought commerce and prosperity, but the sand bars at the river's mouth had been treacherous since before Moses and Stephen F. Austin first yearned for the land on its banks. The jetties stretched into the Gulf of Mexico, protecting shipping but slowing down the river's movement out into ocean waters, so the Brazos deposited a huge load of sand, picked up hundreds of miles away in the mountains of Texas, right at its mouth.

To solve the sandbar problem and make entry into and exit from the Brazos River a sure thing, the Atlantic, Gulf & Pacific Company of New York and Houston was hired in 1928. It dredged a new channel for the Brazos River and built a dam to close off what is now called the Old River. Meanwhile, "The Bridge Built over Dry Land," which was featured in "Ripley's Believe It or Not," was constructed over what would become the new river channel. In 1929, a dredge made the final cut to divert the river into its new channel. Minutes before, the new Highway 36 bridge had hovered over dry ground.

This photogenic and evidently very happy couple are seated in front of the bridge when it was still under construction in 1928. The new bridge symbolized a new era for Freeport and Velasco. The sandbars at the river's mouth, which had plagued shipping for hundreds of years, were about to be defeated. The Old Brazos River and Freeport would be a safe and quiet haven for shipping from around the world. El Rio de los Brazos de Dios could now plunge to the Gulf well downstream from the port and deposit its load of sand there. The economy of Freeport and Velasco would soar, and this unknown couple's fortunes would fly high, too. However, the next year was 1929, the year the diversion channel was finished and the year the bottom dropped out in the Great Depression.

FREEPORT HARBOR,
Showing
River Diversion and Dam
Constructed by ATLANTIC, GULF & PACIFIC CO.

P 85 8.2

These views of the Brazos River from the air in 1929 are mesmerizing. Freeport, on the right above, had grown to be much larger than Velasco, which would fill out later but never quite catch up. The dam is visible toward the bottom. The Old River then winds majestically up and under the bridge built between Velasco and Freeport in 1916, while the diversion channel arrows straight off to the right under the new Highway 36 bridge, which is no longer resting on dry ground. The new mouth of the river is not too far distant at the end of the new channel. The picture below shows the new river mouth. Notice the lack of jetties.

The new Freeport High School was built in the 1930s on West Fourth Street. Many happy students walked through its halls and graduated from this much-loved building. One principal after another made sure each student was getting a good education. The students enjoyed many extracurricular activities, including the 1934 band pictured below. After Brazosport High School was built in the 1960s, this building became Freeport Intermediate School. The building was refurbished with red brick and limestone blocks. Tom Patterson was its principal in the 1980s, and the author taught sixth-grade language arts and reading there for 13 years, until the sixth grade was moved to Lanier Middle School.

Businesses were thriving in Freeport. Bearhunter's Café had originally been located at 610 West First Street at the bridge over the Old Brazos River to Velasco. Then the business was moved to 531 West Second Street, where it is shown above in 1934. The building, which was damaged in the tornado of 1943, later became the Georgian Café. The picture below shows West Second Street in 1938. Harry Wetzel owned the M System Grocery Store. Also shown are Brockman and Co. Dry Goods, the Freeport Theatre, Willenberg's Drugs and Sundries, a furniture store, and a gifts and office supply store.

In the 1930s, the Freeport Pharmacy published the postcard above of the Freeport Community House, which the Freeport Sulphur Company had built on West Second Street. Pristine and beautiful, it hugged the levee and provided access for walks along the Old Brazos River. It still stands and hosts many community events. When World War II broke out, Dow Chemical Company came to town and flooded the area with new employees. Shacks appeared in the hundreds, some along the banks of the Old River. They were an eyesore but were necessary, because Freeport and Velasco could not house the thousands of newcomers.

MAGNESIUM FROM SEA WATER BY ELECTROCHEMISTRY IS A WARTIME REVOLUTION

Just as sulphur originally put Freeport on the map, so magnesium continued the process. The need for the metal for war—for making firebombs, tracer bullets, flares, and in the manufacturing of aircraft—made it immensely valuable. So when Dow Chemical Company decided that Freeport's access to seawater made it the perfect place for its new plant, a new era arrived in Freeport and the area that would become Lake Jackson. Dow began using electrochemistry to extract magnesium from seawater. The process electrified the public's imagination. Pictured are employees being honored for being present when the first magnesium ingot was poured. They are standing in front of stacks of ingots.

Working with liquid sulphur at the Freeport Sulphur Company was so hazardous that the company built a hospital for its workers. Working in the "mag cells" was also extremely dangerous and required care, as seen at right. The picture below shows the first women to work in the Dow plant. They are smiling happily. Working outside of the home was a new thing for married women. Working in industrial plants was brand new. But many of the men had gone to war, and "womanpower" was a shot in the arm for the war effort. "Rosie the Riveter" made that clear.

Above is Dow Chemical Company's Plant B as it appeared from the air in 1949. So severe was the need for magnesium that the US government built the plant when World War II broke out and leased the plant to Dow. After the war was over, Dow bought the federal government out, becoming the full owner on November 19, 1949. During the war, because of Dow's proximity to the Gulf, military protection was necessary, and Army military police are pictured below in 1942 at Dow's Plant A. At the closed-down Freeport Sulphur Company, the three defunct smokestacks could have guided submarines into the Brazos River and straight to Dow, so they were dynamited. (Above, courtesy of the Brazoria County Historical Commission.)

Fishing has been important to the Freeport-Velasco area since the Karankawa Indians traveled its banks. These fish were caught in the 1940s by either commercial or sports fishermen and displayed at Bown Seafoods in Freeport. Shrimping was a huge part of Freeport's economy for decades. The shrimp boats docked side-by-side in the Old Brazos River. A car ride alongside the levee was a pleasure. Seamen on the docked boats tended to their livelihood, repairing nets and machinery. The boats' names were a feast for the imagination.

Sometimes shrimping ran in families, and the Muchowiches were one. One of their shrimp boats was the *Dolphin*, owned by Capt. Carl Muchowich in the late 1930s. It was 42 feet long and had a 145-horsepower engine. It was one of a fleet of boats owned by Captain Carl. In the 1930s, three new boats were added at a cost of $100,000. Clearly, Captain Carl's business was doing well. He is shown at left grading shrimp at his business in Freeport. Joe Charles Muchowich is watching him, with Raymond Muchowich in the background. Both boys were learning the business from the ground up.

Nat Hickey wrote a wonderful booklet describing the origin in 1940 and final resting place of the shrimp boat *Mystery*, shown in the Freeport Municipal Park. "Her origin was a cypress swamp," Hickey wrote. "Her maker was a bayou boat builder named S. Klonaris, who had set up shop on the Louisiana coast. . . . *Mystery* was fashioned from cypress wood by craftsmen who could curve and fit a cypress plank to the sweep of a hull by eyeball measurement. . . . There was never anything glamorous about the *Mystery*. Wide-hulled and solid, she was designed for strength and reliability. She carried bunks for a crew of three, with all remaining space devoted to the task of harvesting, cleaning and storing Gulf Shrimp. . . . She was named *Mystery* because many thought it would be a mystery if the builder could be paid."

Mystery's working life ended when she was 25 years old. About that time, a suggestion of Buster Curry's resulted in the Brazosport Chamber of Commerce's getting to work. It planned to make the *Mystery* into a monument to the shrimping industry that had been so important to Freeport-Velasco. The process of moving *Mystery* from the Old Brazos River to her present berth in the Freeport Municipal Park was arduous, but well worth it. She is a beauty, right by Highway 288 where everyone can see her. Much loved by the community and sightseers, she is decked out gorgeously each Christmas.

Shrimp boats like the *Mystery* shared the Old Brazos River with much bigger ships. The river moved much more calmly since its major diversion-channel operation in 1929. No longer did the "Old Lady" throw mounds of sand into her mouth. Instead, ships could steam quietly through the jetties into the Old Brazos River, past the Philips Tank Farm and Port of Freeport, and on up into Dow Chemical Company's barge canal. Business at Philips, Dow, and the Port of Freeport prospered. Local churches began thinking about all the seamen entering Freeport on their ships. They built a seamen's center that has ministered to seamen's needs for many years. Container trucks moved up Highways 35 and 288 and FM 523 into Texas's great interior, rumbling past businesses and homes in Freeport, Velasco, and Oyster Creek. The economy prospered.

Movie theaters prospered, too. Everyone loved going to the movies, or to "the pictures" or "the show." Popcorn never tasted as good as in a movie theater. In the 1950s, one could buy a Baby Ruth candy bar about a foot long for 5¢. The Showboat and the Ora Theaters were full every weekend in Freeport, along with the Velasco Theater over the river. Viewers sat mesmerized watching the big screen. (Above, courtesy of Charles "Chuck" Ainsworth.)

Before or after the movie, Antonelli's was the place to go. Henry Antonelli opened his root beer and hamburger stand in 1923 in the 1000 block of West Second Street. He never told anyone his secret root beer recipe. People flocked to the stand for decades. When Antonelli passed away, his son gave the stand to the City of Freeport. It was placed in between the *Mystery* and the Freeport Public Library in the Freeport Municipal Park and serves delicious hamburgers and other fast food today. Below, Betty Allen (left) and Shirley Allen Parrot, shown working at the Southwestern Bell Telephone Company switchboard, might have bought a root beer float together after work.

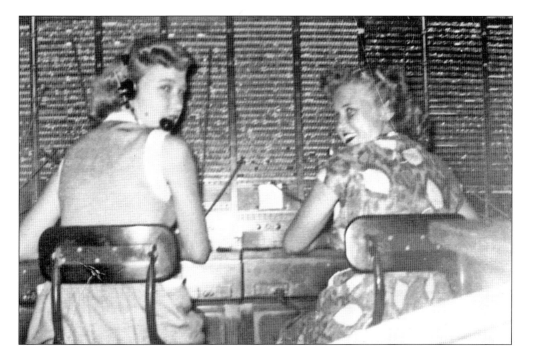

Businesses were thriving all along West Second Street. One was Anthony's Department Store, next to Willenberg's Pharmacy. Alice Woodruff worked there as a sales clerk. Bolts of fabric lining the wall behind her attest to the number of garments made at home by the women of Freeport and Velasco. The city government overseeing all these prosperous businesses was housed in the Freeport City Hall at 128 East Fourth Street, shown below. Palm trees attest to Freeport's mild climate. These pictures were taken in the 1950s, just before Velasco and Freeport consolidated into one town. Suddenly, the Freeport mayor and city council had a lot more work to do.

So did the Freeport Police Department. One of patrolman Carl Linzay's duties in 1955 (two years before consolidation) was to teach bicycle safety to boys and girls. That year, John William Adams, 10 years old and a Freeport fifth-grader, may have participated in the Freeport Jaycees essay contest on safety. He is shown demonstrating a left turn signal on one of two bicycles donated by Sears, Roebuck and Company's local order house. From left to right, Marvin Fields, Tab Brimage, and Patrolman Linzay look on. The picture may have appeared in one of the newspapers published that week by the *Brazosport Facts*, whose building on East Park Avenue in Freeport is shown below.

Freeport's East End has been a close-knit community over the decades. Past and present inhabitants cherish fond memories of the neighborhood and meet for reunions every year. Lila Lloyd is one of the most distinguished East End citizens. The picture above shows, from left to right, Doug Domingues, Denny Waddy, and O'Neil Hudson in the 1960s. At left is an East End cleanup in progress in September 1969. In 2016, the Port of Freeport built housing near its new headquarters and offered East Enders three-bedroom houses. Some took the offer, and some chose to keep their longtime homes.

Every January, Freeport has a lovely parade honoring the birthday of the Rev. Martin Luther King Jr. Often the drum majors, including Lila Lloyd, ride in Freeport's trolley. Other honorees ride in beautiful cars. This festive convertible is blue-black with big red and gold ribbons honoring Dr. King. One year, the Buffalo Soldiers National Museum in Houston sent reenactors to join the parade. Some brought their horses and rode among the many on horseback. Theresa Jackson is one of the many organizers of the parade. She and others spend many hours planning and carrying out this significant community event. The parade begins on Cherry Street and continues down Second Street, which in March 2017 was renamed Martin Luther King Jr. Boulevard.

The Port of Freeport is a major deep-water seaport. It is home to several onsite import-export businesses. Huge ships, like the *Eurytan* of the Marchessini Lines, pictured above in Freeport in the 1990s, move in and out of the port. Eighteen-wheelers haul new vehicles to the port daily to load them onto outgoing ships. Then they load imported cars to take them into Texas's interior. Chiquita and Dole cargo containers are offloaded onto semi-trucks to be transported inland. Two big cranes are visible from across Freeport. The Port of Freeport has moved into an important position in the Texas Gulf Coast economy.

A flood in 1916, exactly 100 years before the great Brazos River flood of 2016, greatly damaged the swing bridge seen above as it was being built between Freeport and Velasco. But it was finished and served Freeport-Velasco for nearly 100 years, first as an auto and railroad bridge, then for the railroad only. In 2010, it was demolished and replaced with the Union Pacific lift bridge shown below. Nostalgic citizens remembered jumping off the railroad tracks leading to the river and hated to see the old bridge go, so a wonderful model of the old swing bridge was built and is housed in the Freeport Historical Museum.

Wanda Jean Hickey remembers when her parents, Bernice and Lee Richardson, opened their Hurricane Glass and Sales Company on Gulf Boulevard in Velasco. They had moved to town in 1942. Lee Richardson worked for Dow and said about the birth of Lake Jackson, "They can't make a town in that gator-infested swamp!" Wanda Jean's mother had been trained in a Fort Worth photography school. They opened Richardson's Photography, the first full-time photography studio in Brazoria County, and did all their own developing in trays in the dark. There was a gift shop in the studio where Wanda Jean remembers getting birth-month angels for her babies. Later, her parents opened Hurricane Glass adjoining the studio. The driver of this Brazos Glass and Mirror Company truck must have been horror-stricken when he drove through the Richardsons' plate glass. Lee Richardson had called his business Hurricane Glass, because, he said, there would always be hurricanes on the Gulf Coast, and people would always need glass. He was a wise man.

Three

HURRICANES AND FLOODS

Water was what put the gleam in Moses and Stephen F. Austin's eyes. The Gulf of Mexico was full of it, and so was the Brazos River. There was easy access (forgetting, for the moment, the sand bars at the river's mouth) for travelers and for commerce. The Austin men and the Old Three Hundred colonists loved all that water.

But water is unruly. It does what it wants to. It turns its back, and there is drought. Or it deluges, and there is flood. The Brazos River has flooded repeatedly since the *Lively* arrived in 1821. Once, the Brazos, Colorado, and San Bernard Rivers met in one vast floodplain. Just recently, the Brazos River flood of 2016 devastated the countryside upstream while sparing Freeport-Velasco.

Hurricanes can be far more devastating than floods. They came roaring in over the Gulf of Mexico so many times in the six decades after Velasco was founded that the villagers moved four miles upstream to New Velasco. They hoped they had found safety, but that was before the hurricane of 1900 hit. Galveston was its main target, but old, damaged, unpublishable pictures of New Velasco taken in 1900 show a rubble-strewn plain where wooden buildings had become matchsticks. The majestic Velasco Hotel and its dance pavilion were smashed to pieces and carried out to sea. A gallon of milk weighs 8.6 pounds. Dropped just right, it can break a toe. How much did the giant, water-filled fist of the Gulf of Mexico weigh? Enough to destroy New Velasco.

Very close to the waters of the Gulf of Mexico, providing a beacon to guide ships through the jetties and into the Brazos River harbor, stood the lighthouse. When a hurricane rolled in from the Gulf, the lighthouse was right in its path. According to J.A. Creighton's article "Narrative History of Brazoria County," published in *SW Historical Quarterly*, the Brazos River lighthouse was first lit on May 30, 1896. It flashed "every five seconds and [was] visible for 15 miles at sea. In 1936 the lamp was converted to electricity and increased to 190,000 candle power. Again in 1963 the candle power was increased to 2,000,000." The ship pictured below was a lighthouse tender in the early 1900s.

The dramatic aerial photograph of the Brazos River lighthouse above was taken on March 11, 1964, shortly before the lighthouse was decommissioned. Many in Freeport-Velasco were heartsick to see the old landmark go. Someone engaged a pilot so they could take a few last pictures. The land had been sold to Dow Chemical Company, and the venerable beacon was carefully dismantled. The prismatic-glass-and-brass lenses, through which the lamp had blazed for six decades, were mounted in an exhibit at the Brazoria County Historical Museum. The photograph at right was taken by the *Brazosport Facts* in 1984.

COAST GUARD STATION, FREEPORT, TEX.

Local history records the destruction of Life Saving Station No. 219 as occurring in 1915. However, the Coast Guard historian's terse remarks state, "1914 a severe storm completely destroyed the buildings and made an island of the site, thereby rendering the site useless for life-saving purposes. Station Freeport is a descendent of this station."

In 1898, two years before the Gulf of Mexico nearly washed New Velasco off the face of the earth, the Brazos River flooded. The big building below was a substantial bank building. It was destroyed in 1900. The people of Velasco were staunch and sturdy. They had to be to endure one watery catastrophe after another and stay put. They either had nowhere else to go or they really loved the Gulf Coast.

This flood hit Velasco in 1913. Snakes' habitats were flooded as well, and they sought shelter in human homes as the flood waters rose. The snakes at left, pictured during that flood, looked for solid, dry ground. There are four kinds of venomous snakes in Texas: cottonmouths, coral snakes, copperheads, and rattlesnakes. Non-venomous snakes greatly outnumber the venomous kind, but they can still scare anyone to death. Finding a rat snake, which can grow to six feet, on one's front porch is enough to give anyone the heebie-jeebies or maybe even a heart attack. A snake bite is always a very serious matter.

Above, Freeport is flooded in 1928, and below, Velasco is flooded in 1929. Each of the twin cities was flooded both years. The Freeport National Bank is on the first floor of the big brick building above, with the Freeport Sulphur Company on the second floor. The flooded buildings in Velasco were much less substantial. In 1928, the Bridge Built over Dry Land was being built, and was finished by 1929. The construction site was flooded and the digging of the diversion channel greatly impeded by the heavily surging Brazos River. Still, the river's destructive power could not match that shown by the Gulf in a hurricane.

This is Velasco, probably after the hurricane of September 8, 1900. It was a Category 4 storm with winds up to 145 miles per hour. It rolled over Galveston, a very low island, from two sides, bringing Galveston's bay waters over it from behind and the Gulf of Mexico from in front. An estimated 6,000 to 12,000 people died there. Velasco's position four miles upstream from the mouth of the Brazos and inland from the Gulf made it much better off than the island city. Still, the storm surge rolled up the Brazos and over Velasco's Avenues A and B. There is no recorded history of what Velasco's citizens did with the little warning they had that a big storm was coming. Most of the buildings were wooden and subject to twisting and ripping by wind and water. What did they do to protect themselves?

The photograph above was taken in Velasco after either the 1909 or 1915 storm. It shows the telephone company in the foreground with a hotel in the background. The photograph below shows Velasco Lodge 757. It was the second Masonic lodge used after the 1900 storm. The Masons were stalwart citizens of Velasco. Their lodge was destroyed again in 1909, but they built again. These pictures show how devastating the nearby Gulf was. But residents were undaunted. They stayed, more than a century ago, and became the forebears of present-day Texans.

The damaged buildings above may have been the ones H. Bascom Simpson saw in 1915 when he arrived in Velasco to begin his job as superintendent of schools. In his memoirs, he wrote of the need to clean out the school building, including evidence that animals had been inside. The image below shows people among the debris left by the 1900, 1909, or 1915 storm. They had enough presence of mind to want to record the evidence that, while their town had been blown to pieces, they were calm and collected and would rebuild.

On August 14, 1932, a hurricane blasted Freeport-Velasco. Nat Hickey, who was nine years old that year, said that the winds were the worst he has ever experienced. Pictured above are the effects of those winds on the Freeport Community House. Note the table and forlorn piano. Technology had advanced quite a bit since the 1900, 1909, and 1915 hurricanes. People were given enough warning to flee, and they did. Below, the automobile parked near the funeral home run by the Friedrich family stayed. The telephone exchange is in the center, and the Freeport City Barn is on the right.

It is hard to tell that this was Ford Gulf Motor Sales. Many of the people who fled from this huge hurricane may have been riding in Fords. Model As and Model Ts were some of the first automobiles sold in Freeport-Velasco, maybe by someone related to the owner of this dealership. No one knows whether anyone was in these buildings when the great winds picked them up and reassembled them. Had the salesmen and office staff fled in their own cars? They would have gone over the swing bridge to Velasco or up and over the Bridge Built over Dry Land.

Car dealerships did not fare too well during the big storm. These two photographs show Lynn Chevrolet. It was built of brick in the 200 block of Broad Street, right in the middle of thriving businesses. Men and women had poured their hearts into their livelihoods on Broad Street. They had remained again and again as one storm after another tore their work apart. But we are so much smaller than millions of gallons of water and so tiny compared to 150-mile-per-hour winds pushing that water.

One important form of livelihood was the rooming house or boardinghouse. H. Bascom Simpson lived in a boardinghouse for a while after he moved to Velasco. Mary Ella Duck ran the pictured one long before apartments made her business obsolete. She would have washed her boarders' bed linens the hard way, by hand. Providing them hot breakfasts and suppers every day, seven days a week, with work-roughened hands and an aching back, was work she was no doubt grateful for—hard, honest, work during the Great Depression, when many had no work. What happened to Mary Ella Duck's business in 1932 is unknown. It is known what happened to Carroll's Rooming House, which was right next door to Lynn Chevrolet.

Hopefully, the boarders and workers in Carroll's Rooming House had packed up into an automobile and crossed one of Freeport's two bridges out of town. The terrible winds of the unnamed hurricane picked up the wooden building and tossed it into the air, crashing it against Lynn Chevrolet's solid brick mass. The boardinghouse was pulled apart and stripped of all the furnishings Rachel Carroll had carefully acquired. The galvanized washing tubs and kitchen utensils, food stocked up in the pantry, and linens carefully cleaned and stacked in closets were strewn to the wind. The sun came out and looked down through vacant windows into the bare, ruined building.

Unlike the wooden rooming house, this building was stone. The winds evidently attacked the roof. No one knows exactly how its forces converged on the covering of this carefully built, hope-filled business. The owner must have made the plans just so and watched lovingly as his business was built. Maybe, like the Tobeys, who built their second hardware building at the corner of East Park Avenue and West Second Street in the early 1900s, he constructed some of it with his own hands. He certainly never dreamed that the roof would be removed so precipitously and tons of water poured into the second floor. That water pushed against the wall, whose supports had been removed in one corner of the building, and shoved the stone out of place. A car and a truck are parked outside the building as recovery has begun.

The storm winds whirled down Broad Street, ricocheting from one side to another, carrying debris from wooden buildings like Carroll's Rooming House. Two-by-fours scythed through the air, a terrible danger to anyone outside. After the angry winds subsided and people returned to town, they walked around, dazed, trying to decide which board to pick up first. In the residential area pictured below, the gale had torn the roof off one side of a house and removed its garage. Next to a smashed house in the foreground, a bathtub lies forlornly on its side, waiting for its dismayed owners to set it upright.

Many houses in Freeport-Velasco were destroyed in 1932. Above is T.H. Brand's house after the storm. Half of the roof is gone, along with the upper part of the chimney and untold numbers of shingles. Below is Sagness Girouard's house at 513 West Broad Street. One year before the hurricane, in 1931, a railroad underpass had been dug out next to Girouard's Ace Hardware Store on West Second Street. The fill dirt was transported to the family home to help protect it from rising water. No one dreamed of the high winds that would come screaming out of the Gulf of Mexico the very next year.

The man above looks bemused and perplexed. If he was the owner of the building behind him, he was in a lot of trouble. Even if he just worked there, he had a real, personal stake in getting the business going again in the middle of the Great Depression. The water would take a while to subside, and after that, the serious work would begin. The photograph below shows another business, the Freeport Sulphur Drug Store. This one would have taken much longer to get back into shape. It was a long time before Freeport-Velasco fully recovered from the hurricane of 1932.

Freeport-Velasco had nine years to rebuild before the next big unnamed hurricane arrived on September 23, 1941. The Texas State Historical Association's *Texas Almanac*, in its summary, "Significant Weather, 1940s," reports: "Sept. 23, 1941: Hurricane. Center moved inland near Matagorda and passed over Houston about midnight. Extremely high tides along coast in the Matagorda to Galveston area. . . . Four lives lost. Damage was $6.5 million." This boat, affected by those "extremely high tides," was washed up onto the Velasco levee. Many boats were docked in the Old Brazos River in 1941, and this was probably not the only one with a new berth.

CITIES $29,830.00
ROADS 1,500.00
AGRICULTURE 3,500.00

TOTAL LOSSES $34,830.00

IMPROVEMENTS REQUIRED TO PREVENT
RECURRENCE $15,000.00

SHADED AREA WAS INUNDATED

LIMIT OF CARLA'S TIDEWATER 15 ELEVATION

LAKE JACKSON $1,800,000
BASTROP $1,900,000
RICHWOOD $2,620,000
CLUTE $2,750,000
LAKE BARBARA $1,300,000
JONES CREEK $960,000
OYSTER CREEK $4,000,000
FREEPORT $14,500,000

Twenty years went by. In 1953, the practice of giving names to hurricanes began. Then, on September 11, 1961, Hurricane Carla, a Category 5 hurricane with 115-mile-per-hour winds at Matagorda and 88-mile-per-hour winds at Galveston, swarmed up the Texas Gulf Coast. The pictured "Survey Report on the Effect of Hurricane Carla in Brazoria County, Texas," a 1961 Brazoria County publication, records $14,500,000 worth of damage in Freeport alone. The National Weather Service said, on the fiftieth anniversary of Hurricane Carla, "Carla was the most intense hurricane to make landfall on the Texas coast in the 20th century and second in recorded history only to the Indianola hurricane of 1886." This includes the great Galveston hurricane of 1900. Some hurricanes have had higher winds, including probably the storm of 1932. What was so destructive about Carla was the storm surge, which, according to the report, "was the highest in hurricane history along the Texas coast, rising 10 feet above normal along a 300 mile swath."

When a hurricane pushes untold millions of tons of water inland at an abnormal height called a storm surge, it does enormous damage. Hurricane Carla carried the Gulf of Mexico across Freeport, up into parts of Lake Jackson, over Oyster Creek, and all the way into the outskirts of Angleton. These aerial photographs of the countryside and roadways show how far the water moved. The author was attending Bellaire High School in Houston, 50 miles inland from Galveston. School was out for several days all the way up there, and a tree fell down in her yard, having been twisted and corkscrewed by Carla's winds.

The World Meteorological Organization began assigning female names to hurricanes in 1953, with men's names added in 1978. Six lists of names are rotated, so that, for example, the 1996 set was used again in 2002. No one on the Texas Gulf Coast will soon forget the hurricane named Carla. These photographs were taken near Jane Long Elementary School, probably in the same neighborhood as the cover image.

After Hurricane Carla, the Velasco Drainage District had had enough. In *Velasco Drainage District, 1908–1991*, Ralph W. Gilbert stated that, realizing that the hurricane protection and levee system had to be improved, the district did make improvements costing nearly $17 million. In 1978, "The Army Corps of Engineers completed a large tidal control structure in the Old Brazos River which prevents high tide levels." This is the structure variously known as the "tide gate," "the H," or "the guillotine." It is a beautiful, heart-tugging sight visible across town. Below is the view from the top looking down after Hurricane Allen in August 1980, with flotsam washed up at the foot of the tide gate. (Both, courtesy of the *Brazosport Facts*.)

No one wanted to see Gilbert come to town, but in September 1988, it did. Students at Freeport Intermediate School were beside themselves when school was dismissed from Wednesday through Friday. Teachers felt a little different because of three lost days of class. But everyone fled in the face of the Category 5 storm. It caused so much damage in its nine-day life—318 lives lost and damages exceeding $7.1 billion along its path—that the name was retired in the spring of 1989 and replaced with Gordon.

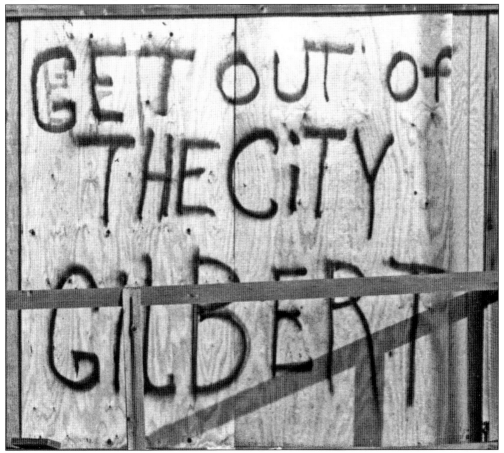

Seventeen years after Gilbert, Category 5 Katrina terrified the Gulf Coast on August 29, 2005, killing 1,836 and causing $90.9 billion in damage. When Rita arrived less than a month later, becoming a Category 5 storm on September 21, a massive flight occurred. The deaths and damages were less than Katrina, and everyone returned home subdued but relieved. Three years later, Hurricane Ike was quite a different matter. Texans fled in the largest evacuation in the state's history. When they returned, the National Guard brought food and water to residents. School was out in Freeport for a week. In Lake Jackson, a great number of lovely old trees were blown down, leaving many without electricity for three weeks. Neighbors got to know each other as they cooked together outside. When Surfside residents tried to return home, they met the pictured roadblocks. Once home, some found their vehicles half-buried in water.

Surfside was hit very hard. Many beach houses were destroyed and their contents strewn across the island. Galveston Island's John Sealy Hospital was severely damaged. The Flagship Hotel, memorable for being built out on a pier, was left with a big hole in one wall, as if a giant wrecking ball had knocked out a big chunk. Bolivar Peninsula looked from the air as if a monstrous windshield-wiper had raked all the houses off it. Displaced students moved in with relatives, some in Freeport. Many were stunned and vulnerable after the great storm destroyed their homes overnight.

Freeport-Velasco is buffered from the Gulf of Mexico by the island of Quintana. After Hurricane Ike, water had submerged parts of the bridge into Quintana. The water effectively marooned Quintana residents for a time. The photograph below shows Ike's damage to the Coveney House in Quintana Beach Park. It was built sometime in the 1880s, while the Seaburn shipyard was stimulating the economy and Quintana was flourishing as a shipping community. The Seaburn house, built in the 1840s, and the Coveney house have endured for decades and have withstood all the hurricanes mentioned in this book. They stand even now.

One reason Freeport-Velasco has been able to keep coming back for more is the tide gate, visible in 2016 under the Pine Street Bridge. The massive gate lumbers down to the river bed whenever a storm surge threatens. Storm surges are devastating. Hurricane Katrina's storm surge, the highest recorded in US history at 27.5 feet, killed many people and destroyed many lives. Together with the levee system, the tide gate protects the boats moored at the Freeport Marina. The lovely craft lie safely moored and move gently at anchor when other boats motor up the Old Brazos River past the marina. The dry dock building is huge. Sleek beauties are lifted up to storage with a monstrous rolling lift. Members of the Houston Yacht Club sail down and dock their boats at the marina for events like the Texas Billfish Championship. Along with other City of Freeport entities, the Freeport Marina makes Freeport-Velasco's future shine as bright as the sun on the gently rolling river. (Both, courtesy of Dan Kessner.)

Here is the *Mystery* in 2016. She lived through many years as a working shrimp boat and still looks chipper and alert after decades of being one of the best-loved monuments in Freeport. Residents and tourists drive by on Highway 288 and slow down to check her out. She is decked out in Christmas lights every year, along with all of the nearby Freeport Municipal Park. Antonelli's, also beloved by area residents, sits right alongside the shrimp boat and sells really good hamburgers. Close by is the Freeport Public Library and the beautiful Veterans Memorial, established in 2007. (Both, courtesy of Dan Kessner.)

The City of Freeport Museum, also known as the Freeport Historical Museum, was built as the Masonic lodge in the early 1900s. The photograph below, of what was originally the Freeport National Bank and Freeport Sulphur Company building and is now privately owned, was taken from the second-floor balcony of the Freeport Historical Museum. The two buildings have kept each other company for over 100 years. They withstood every hurricane from the early 1900s on. They lived through the happy, hectic years when Freeport was a thriving commercial center and shoppers passed their doors many times a day. Now they are watching the rebirth of downtown Freeport. (Both, courtesy of Dan Kessner.)

The Freeport Police Department is built up high to keep it functional during high water. Mandatory evacuations have been necessary during the most severe hurricanes, and the police department has stood through them all. Dan Pennington was the chief of police until August 2017, when he moved to San Antonio. Capt. Ray Garivey heads up the Criminal Investigation Division and SWAT, while Capt. Danny Gilchriest is over patrol. The police department conducts an excellent citizens police academy each year. Because of the Freeport Police Department and other hard-working city agencies, former mayor Norma Moreno Garcia, current mayor Troy Brimage, city council, and city manager Jeff Pynes and his staff, Freeport is heading steadily into a flourishing and prosperous future. (Both, courtesy of Dan Kessner.)

The Freeport trolley is the caboose of this book. The author, pictured at right, delighted in driving the trolley from 2011 to 2016. Driving the trolley is a little like riding with Miss America. Children and adults stand and watch, waving happily, as the only Freeport monument on wheels rolls by. The trolley carried brides to their weddings and three-year-old birthday boys and their guests to visit the fire department and police department. It took part in the Freeport Little League, the Brazosport High School homecoming, and the Martin Luther King parades. It ferried people from the parking lot across Highway 288, past the dear old *Mystery* and Antonelli's, down into the Freeport Municipal Park pavilion for the Cinco de Mayo celebration and the Rotary shrimp boil, and to River Place for the Thanksgiving SuperFeast and the Freeport Police Department's Blue Santa event. It even took Santa and Mrs. Claus to Freeport's Christmas celebration and the Easter Bunny to Brazos Mall. The Freeport trolley is a lovely lady, as is the 105-year-old town it represents. May it and Freeport-Velasco live long and be very, very happy. (Above, author's collection; right, courtesy of Yolanda Hernandez-Mejia.)

DISCOVER THOUSANDS OF LOCAL HISTORY BOOKS
FEATURING MILLIONS OF VINTAGE IMAGES

Arcadia Publishing, the leading local history publisher in the United States, is committed to making history accessible and meaningful through publishing books that celebrate and preserve the heritage of America's people and places.

Find more books like this at
www.arcadiapublishing.com

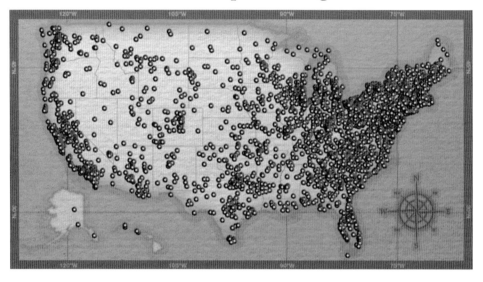

Search for your hometown history, your old stomping grounds, and even your favorite sports team.

Consistent with our mission to preserve history on a local level, this book was printed in South Carolina on American-made paper and manufactured entirely in the United States. Products carrying the accredited Forest Stewardship Council (FSC) label are printed on 100 percent FSC-certified paper.

MADE IN THE

USA